Science in Our World

by Zachary Cohn

PEARSON
Scott
Foresman

How do farmers use technology to grow food?

Food comes from many places.

Food comes from lakes.

Food comes from animals.

Food comes from farms.

Machines help farmers.

Machines are technology.

Technology is using science to solve problems.

Technology changes with time.

Planting and Growing Corn

The farmer plows the soil.

The plow makes the job easier.

The plow is technology.

The soil is ready to plant.

The farmer plants seeds.

The farmer uses a seed drill.

A seed drill is technology.

It makes the work go faster.

How does food get from the farm to the store?

The corn plants grow.

The farmer picks the corn.

This is called a harvest.

Machines help the farmer.

The corn is ready to sell.

It is put on a truck.

The truck takes the corn to the store.

What tools can you use to make dinner?

People use tools.

Tools make work easier.

Each tool is used for a different job.

Serving Dinner

We need tools to make dinner.

What will you use?

A spoon can lift the meat.

Tongs can pick up lettuce.

How do builders get wood for a house?

Workers used axes long ago.

Now they use machines.

One machine cuts the trees.

One moves the heavy logs.

Moving Logs to the Sawmill

This machine picks up the logs.

It places them on the truck.

The truck goes to the mill.

The logs are cut in the mill.

What are simple machines?

People use simple machines.

A **simple machine** is a tool.

It has few or no moving parts.

Simple machines help do jobs.

A **wedge** is a simple machine.

It pushes things apart.

A **wheel and axle** is a simple machine.

It moves things.

This wheelbarrow has a wheel and axle.

This shovel is a wedge.

Using Simple Machines

A **screw** holds things together.

A **lever** lifts things.

A **pulley** moves things up
and down.

An **inclined plane** has one high
end and one low end.

What can you use to communicate?

Technology is used to communicate.

Computers help us communicate.

How do you communicate with people?

Glossary

inclined plane   a simple machine that is high at one end and low at the other end

lever   a simple machine that is used to lift something

pulley   a simple machine that uses a wheel and rope to move things up and down

screw   a simple machine that is used to hold things together

simple machine   a tool with few or no moving parts that makes work easier

technology   the use of scientific knowledge to solve problems

wedge   a simple machine that is used to push things apart

wheel and axle   a simple machine that is used to move things